An Ancient New Born

Thomas Angear

BookLeaf
Publishing

India | USA | UK

Presentation by *BookLeaf Publishing*

Web: www.bookleafpub.com

E-mail: info@bookleafpub.com

ISBN:9789358315264

First edition 2024

DEDICATION

Sandra Florence Russell & Charles William Angear

My late mother and Father who I hope would have enjoyed these scrawlings.

Mirth

Twirling around the old piano

Kicking the legs on a wooden soaked floor

Steamy smiles seen through frosty windows
from visible breathers

Stamping and shouting or singing and stomping

Gravy wine reaches the wardrobes in bedrooms
soon to be burst into

This night is special, time is no matter

Bursting love seeps into the oak, rich with
generational, beautiful years

Painted grins and painted tongues blur

A groom covered in patting cheers whilst a bride
is kissing, joyous tears

Letting the grass grow

2

Lawnmower sits in the shed whilst the grass
dances with glee

Bees gladly bumbling and thanking me

Man

3

Who is this man I am not; I am not changed

Not the pillar of marble or granite

But I am compassionate in the face of doubt

I can change the minds of the angry

Keep the peace when it all seems pointless

I am not granite or marble but more like
mercury, fluid and mercurially unstable

Hannibal

4

I am to cross this mountain

One hundred thousand men at my back

My trunk is heavy

Along with the soldiers sacks

My job is to dredge and pull for my General

Rome is beyond for loss or victory

If we make it; I may not return to my warm
desert home

Walk

5

Pieces of water run into my pockets

My shoes slip-slap in a pace of an untuned
march; lights of cars go by, warm in their tiny
wheeled houses

Highlights

The hard part is pinpointing the highlights of a
mediocre life; falling back off a hill into my
falling bike, leg stuck in chain yelping with
surprise and pain

Parents face as of my first school play, in a sea
of expecting, gleeful others

Or finding out Father Christmas was you all
along

Memory

You were embraced and cherished by all in your
life

A glowing presence that vibrated through
decades of enjoyment, dreams of glowing
nightlife

Along the promenades of sunsets and rises is
almost a ghostly chant of laughter and homely
prizes

You were a figure of concrete strength never to
fall, to negative, but stern surprises

Above the hob

Love tremendously

Talk softly

Drink joyfully

Dance willfully

Walk meanderingly

Hug tightly

Fight justly

Win graciously

Lose graciously

Use sparingly

Journey innocently

and

Live wonderfully

little buddies

a pair sits in the wardrobe stained with mirth,
they've seen the laughs, the falls, the walks
they've seen it all

a pairs sit in the porch covered with marks, the
wisdom, the excitement, the dirt they've seen
my nephew grow tall

a pair sit on the floor embellished with words,
all the tales, the woes, the wiley jokes, they
probably belong in a library as now they are too
small

Too much

Robert Smith issued a statement

The country of Sakandine issued a statement

Suthsexe police force issued statement

I see too many apologies and tenuous words

I'm not involved in this so I'll be sitting over here, away from the absurd

Dark ancient monsters emerge from age old conflicts seen through brand new screens

Some events

Should not be seen

Robert was unfaithful and now we get an earful

He is a stranger

A man created for entertainment for our sustainment during periods of depressing containment

But you can put your phone down and try not to drown, turning the frown upside down

Be there

Remembering the good times can be as tough as
the bad

It makes you think why even remember them at
all, blocking them out

I don't want to remember or block out, I want
move through and move with the memory as it
grows into something new

Processing is too mechanical, I want to be
biological

And bud from trauma

They're not there anymore but you are

A testament to their strength, a testament to their
will to bring you into this world so the world can
be yours

You have life, so live it

XR zay zay zay

I met an alien the other day

His name was jay

And he was from XR zay zay zay

He was really polite

There was no need to fight

He was a massive fan of guacamole

I said 'what brings you to earth?'

He said 'I took a wrong turn and I'm missing my
son's birth'

I said 'well that's no good, you should probably
get back'

He said 'could you do me a favour? My ship is
busted and I need a new engine rack.

Do you know anyone who could sort that?'

'No problem' I said 'I'll call John the mechanic'

John fixed the ship and off Jay went

You're the first person I've told so keep it to
yourself, I don't want to cause panic

To do

16

I like to think I keep on top of it

All the things below are done

Exercise done

Paperwork done

Taxes done

Student loans done

Credit checks done

None of all, have been fun

Benches

17

Straw, wood, grass and pat

A road sleeks down the town where we sat

Families are greeted, jobs undertaken

All under the watch of a pub, as their plunder
will be taken

Ponded mallards squark for a meal

You wanted to sit so our feet could heal

Bikes whip through on the early morning test

Whilst a bird makes a humble yet motherly nest

Life of the spring is new and unfounded

I write to you and say 'please here let our roots
be fully grounded'

On the wall

18

In the frame we smoke and smile, viewing the
cliffs of home

Beautiful you

Smash through the ordinary you

You are perfect and meaningful, a beautiful
muse

Iconography spills when drink, think all your
power strength

Because you are special at being you, maybe just
a lyric is needed to push you into you

Roll

20

Roll Green Hills with dripping sunlight

Roll Green Hills in lovely delight

Roll Green Hills in whatever way you choose

You are mine and for you, I shan't lose

The Game

Crowding into crumbling old arenas

Where the youth and the old blend their years

A hand rubbing and shoulder squeezing
excitement that is felt only here

There may be tears both in glee and in woeful
fears

Burgers, pies and sausage rolls glugged down
with some bovril or local beer

You cherish the numbers like idols of faith

As heroes and villains take the centre stage

A joyful dance of skill and stamina breathe into
the gleaming, devouring eyes

Clouds or sun make no difference, anticipation is
vibrating through old stands

The game is about to begin

Envelope

Snow rare as as a flying pig, a tree that brightens
a low lit lounge

A rose bush with nubs freezing like the
pavement, the postman is off for this one jolly
occasion

The City

The relic stands with dark, upward shooting legs
in the sea

White Indian domes arise from a modest
skyline, esplanade buzzing with family chatter
brisk-fully walking in the salty air and ocean
spatter

Home is south, a rough channel sided with
vineyards and ancient feuds

Thunder may roll and waves crash, cliffs but
home is home and that's what matters

Reach

There is a window in the corner and I can't seem
to reach it

Sunsets, trees, hills, oceans

My bed is long, too long to reach the end, too
long to roll out, too long to stretch my feet

I am stuck inside the wardrobe with nothing to
wear or find, no coats, no shirts, no trousers

The keyhole is my lantern with dusty feet and
mind

My plant withers whilst phone rings it's like
they are combined